CANDLES
FOR BEGINNERS
TO MAKE

Alice Gilbreath

illustrated by Jenni Oliver

William Morrow and Company
New York 1975

Library of Congress Cataloging in Publication Data

Gilbreath, Alice Thompson.
  Candles for beginners to make.

  SUMMARY: Detailed instructions for making many different kinds of
candles.
    1. Candlemaking—Juvenile literature.
[1. Candlemaking] I. Oliver, Jenni, illus.
II. Title.
TT896.5.G54   745.59'3   74-14968
ISBN 0-688-22010-X
ISBN 0-688-32010-4 (lib. bdg.)

By the Same Author

Making Costumes for Parties, Plays, and Holidays

Spouts, Lids, and Cans
  Fun with Familiar Metal Objects

Contents

With love
to my husband, Rex,
who helped with the research
and encouraged me all the way.

Introduction

Candle making is one of the oldest home crafts and was developed in order to have light in the home.

A candle is made from a wick and some type of oil. When the wick is lighted, the oil provides fuel. At first, animal fats were used in candles, but they had an unpleasant odor. Beeswax made better candles, but only the wealthy could afford them. Then, at about the time of the American Civil War, paraffin was developed. It burned with a bright flame, had almost no odor, and made a very satisfactory candle. Later stearin was added as a stiffener to improve it even more. In time, more and more candles began to be made in factories by machines, as well as at home.

As kerosene, gas lamps, and electric lights came into use, candles were no longer needed for lighting homes. But since candles give off a softer light than lamps and electric lights, they have continued to be used for special lighting effects in homes, schools, and restaurants. They are also used for ceremonies and holiday occasions, and for religious services.

Each year more and more candles are sold. Today we can buy candles in many interesting shapes and colors. Some are dipped, some rolled, but most are molded. Some are scented. And candle making as a home craft has continued, for there is a creative challenge in designing and making candles.

Simple and very satisfying, candle making is a popular hobby for all ages; for many people it has become a life-long hobby. This book will get you started. Use it as a guide. If you don't have the color or mold suggested, use what you have that pleases you. Think of your own variations. And have fun making and burning the candles!

Safety Rules. Be sure an adult is in the room with you when you melt or pour wax. Wax is a fuel and can catch fire at very high temperatures. In making all candles, follow these rules:

1. Always set the can containing the wax in a pan one-fourth full of water, and melt the wax over very low heat. Never put the can of wax on direct heat.

2. Fill the can only half full of wax so none can spill.

3. Do not pour wax near heat or an open flame. Turn off the heat before you remove the can for pouring or beating, and use a potholder to handle the hot wax can.

Preparation. Spread several layers of newspaper in your work area. If wax should spill on the counter or floor, let it harden and remove it with a spatula. A one-pound can, such as a coffee can, and a pan of water to set the can in are needed for each different color of wax. You may want a shallow pan of cold water in which to set molds to speed hardening. Hardening can also be hastened by setting the molds in the refrigerator.

Wax. Like many other products, wax is not as plentiful

as it once was. You should have no difficulty in buying candle wax from hobby shops or paraffin from grocery stores, but you should also save stub candles, birthday candles, and used paraffin so you can recycle them into new candles. For making the candles in this book, all kinds of wax can be used. Stub candles should be used to make a candle similar in color to the original one.

Chopping Wax. A board, such as a breadboard, and a sharp knife are needed for chopping wax. Lay the wax chunks or stub candles on the board, and chop with the full length of the knife blade. Keep your fingers well out of the way. Chop until the wax chunks are about a half-inch square, but also use all shavings made while chopping the wax. The chopped wax listed for each candle will be about half that amount when melted.

Melting Wax. Bend a one-pound can, such as a coffee can, on one side to form a spout. Put the wax chunks in the can, and set the can in a pan of water. Melt the wax over *very low* heat. Be sure an adult is in the room with

you when you melt wax. Wax is ready to pour as soon as it is melted. Do not heat further. Be sure to use a pot-holder to handle the hot wax can.

Pouring Wax. Turn the heat off, and move the can of wax to the working area. Pour the wax into the mold. Never pour wax near heat or open flame. Be sure an adult is in the room with you when you pour wax. Wells may form in the center of the candle as it hardens. These may be filled, if you wish, by remelting the wax and pouring it into the well.

Color. Besides old colored candle stubs, pieces of crayon with paper removed are fine for coloring wax. Use at least one and a half inches of a three-eighth-inch-diameter crayon for each cup of chopped white wax. Let the crayon melt along with the wax, and stir the mixture. Add more crayon of the same color if you wish a darker shade.

Wicks. Ordinary cotton twine can be used for wicks. For candles with a diameter of three fourths of an inch or less, use a ten-ply cotton twine. For candles with diameters of more than three fourths of an inch, use a larger cotton twine such as thirty-six ply. Wicking may be purchased at craft stores if you prefer. Use the size wick recommended on the package for the diameter of the candle you are making.

Hold the tip of the twine with your fingers as you dip it in the wax to make the wick. In the instructions for each candle, two inches have been allowed for finger room while dipping. This can be trimmed off when the candle is finished. Pipe cleaners or a plastic straw with a diameter of one eighth of an inch can be used to make a hole for the wick. While the wax is soft, make a hole with the pipe cleaner or plastic straw and insert the wick. A plastic straw is used when it must remain in the wax until the candle has hardened. When the plastic straw is pulled out, it leaves a perfectly round hole, and the wick is easily inserted. If a hole made by either a straw or pipe cleaner is too large for the wick, it will fill in with wax the first time the candle is lighted.

Molds. Sturdy disposable cups—of paper or styrofoam —and milk cartons are good molds because they can be peeled off the candle. China cups or cut-off plastic bottles are good to use if coated inside with cooking oil. Almost any sturdy container that is at least as wide all the way up as it is at the bottom can be coated with cooking oil and used. If cardboard boxes are used, reinforce the seams on the outside with masking tape.

Burning Candles. Always set your candle on a small dish to burn it.

Dip Candle

A good group project

Materials:
chopped wax, any color, 7¾ cups
10-ply cotton twine, 11 inches

Tools:
46-ounce juice can
pan of water
cutting board
sharp knife
scissors

Steps:
1. Put the wax pieces in the can. Set the can in a pan of water, and melt the wax over very low heat. Be sure an adult is in the room with you when you melt or pour wax. Turn the heat off.
2. Measure the depth of the wax in the can, and measure off the same length along the twine. Tie a knot. (Figure 1). Dip the twine in the wax to the knot. Allowing at least five seconds between dippings, dip again and again. A small candle (three eighths of an inch in diameter at the largest point) will require

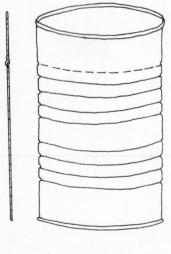

fig. 1

about 125 dips. If this is a group project, let each person dip in turn.

3. The candle will be thick in the center and tapered at both ends. If you
wish two very short candles, lay the
candle on a board and cut it in the center with a sharp knife. If you wish one
longer candle, cut farther down the
thick part and save the remainder for
another project (Figure 2). Dip the
candle or candles one more time. Let
them harden. Cut off the knot and excess wick.

4. Before lighting your dip candle, drip
a few drops of wax in the center of a
saucer and stand the candle in the
warm wax, or place it in a taper holder.

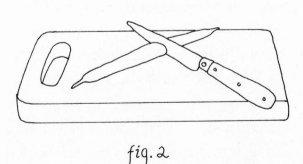

fig. 2

Flower Floater

Materials:
chopped white wax, 3 tablespoons
⅜ inch of yellow crayon
1-inch piece of a birthday candle

Tools:
1-pound can, such as a coffee can,
   bent to form spout
pan of water
a circle of heavy aluminum foil,
   4 inches in diameter
juice glass, 2 to 3 inches in diameter

Steps:
1. Put the wax pieces and crayon in the can. Set the can in a pan of water, and melt the wax over very low heat. Be sure an adult is in the room with you when you melt or pour wax.
2. Lay the foil on a flat surface, and turn up all edges half an inch (Figure 1). Pour the wax on the foil. Let it cool until it is thick but still soft.
3. Press the top of the juice glass into the wax, and twist gently to cut a circle (Figure 2). When the wax is cool enough to handle with your hands, peel

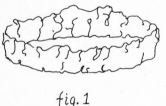

fig. 1

12

away the excess wax around the circle.

4. With your fingers, mold the edges of the wax gently up like the petals of a flower (Figure 3). Stand the inch-long piece of a birthday candle in the center. (If you prefer, lift the wax from the foil and mold the flower petals down instead of up to make a differently shaped flower.) Let it harden.

5. Float the candle in a bowl of water and light it.

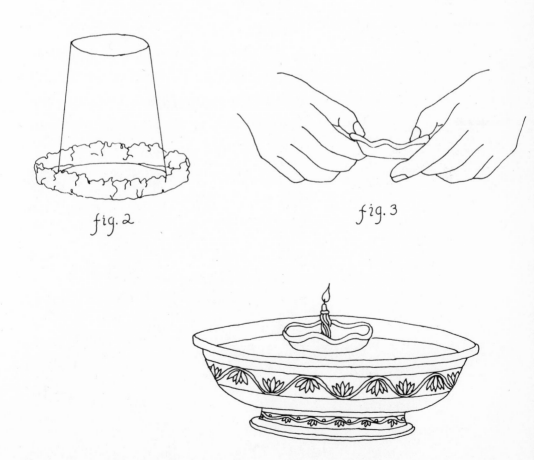

fig. 2

fig. 3

Smile Candle

Materials:
chopped white wax, 1 cup
1½ inches of yellow crayon
36-ply cotton twine, 4 inches
paint, black water-base acrylic
    or half-and-half mixture of
    black tempera paint and
    white glue, such as Elmer's Glue-All

Tools:
1-pound can, such as a coffee can,
    bent to form spout
pan of water
heavy aluminum foil, 1 foot square
pipe cleaner
watercolor paintbrush
scissors

Steps:
1. Put the wax pieces and crayon in the can. Set the can in a pan of water, and melt the wax over very low heat. Be sure an adult is in the room with you when you melt or pour wax.
2. Dip the twine in the wax, and lay it straight on a flat surface to harden. This is the wick.

3. Lay the foil on a flat surface, and turn up all edges half an inch (Figure 1). Pour the wax on the foil. Let it thicken and cool enough so you can work it with your hands. Pull the wax up at the edges, and mold it into a ball.

4. Make a hole with the pipe cleaner through the entire candle at the center of the top (Figure 2). Insert the wick in the hole. Place the candle in the refrigerator to finish hardening.

5. Trim off the excess wick.

6. Paint eyes and a smiling mouth. Let the paint dry.

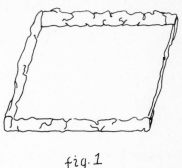

fig. 1

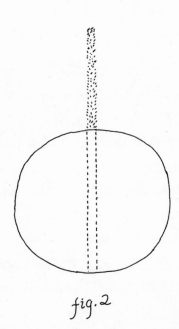

fig. 2

Frosted Candle

Materials:
chopped white wax, 2½ cups
3¾ inches of a brightly colored crayon
36-ply cotton twine, 6 inches

Tools:
1-pound can, such as a coffee can,
  bent to form spout
pan of water
9-ounce disposable cup
pipe cleaner
table fork
table knife or spatula
scissors

Steps:
1. Put the wax and crayon in the can. Set the can in a pan of water, and melt the wax over very low heat. Be sure an adult is in the room with you when you melt or pour wax.
2. Dip the twine in the wax, and lay it straight on a flat surface to harden. This is the wick.
3. Fill the cup three-fourths full of wax. Let it cool until it is thick but still soft.
4. With a pipe cleaner, make a hole

down through the center of the cup to the bottom (Figure 1). Insert the wick in the hole. Let the candle harden. Peel off the cup.

5. Remelt the remaining wax in a pan of water over very low heat. Be sure to turn the heat off, and remove the can of wax to the working area.

6. Beat the wax gently with a fork until it is frothy. Spread on the sides of the candle (and top if you wish) with a table knife or spatula (Figure 2). Cut off the excess wick.

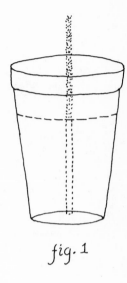

fig. 1

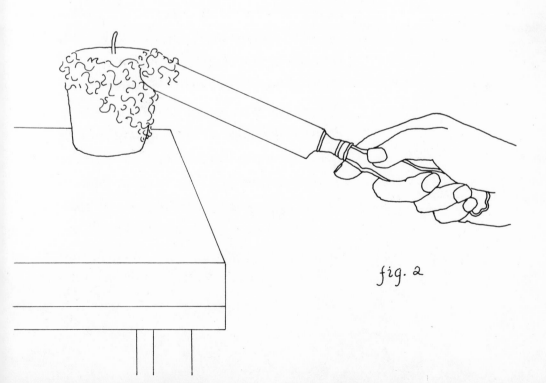

fig. 2

Rainbow Candle

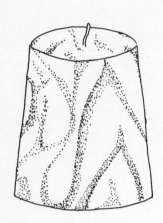

Materials:
chopped white wax, 1½ cups
1 inch each of
    yellow, orange, and purple crayons
36-ply cotton twine, 5 inches

Tools:
4 1-pound cans, such as coffee cans,
    each bent to form spout
3 pans of water
3 pieces heavy aluminum foil,
    each 5 inches square
5-ounce disposable cup
plastic straw, ⅛ inch in diameter
scissors

Steps:
1. Put about one fourth of the wax into each can. Add a different colored crayon piece to each of three cans. Leave the wax in the fourth can white.
2. Put the cans containing crayons in pans of water, and melt the mixtures over very low heat. Be sure an adult is in the room with you when you melt or pour wax.
3. Lay the foil on a flat surface, and

18

turn up all edges of each sheet half an inch (Figure 1). Pour wax of one color onto each piece of foil. Let them harden.

4. Break the colored wax into large pieces, and stand them up in the cup. Let the pieces reach almost to the top of the cup. Mix the colors well.

5. Stand the drinking straw up in the center of the cup by wedging it between pieces of wax. Be certain it reaches the bottom of the cup. (Figure 2).

6. Set the can of white wax in a pan of water, and melt over very low heat. Dip the twine in the wax, and lay it straight on a flat surface to harden. This is the wick.

7. Pour the remaining wax into the cup containing the colored wax pieces. Let it harden.

8. Peel off the disposable cup. Move the straw gently up and down a few times, and remove it. Turn the candle upside down.

9. Put the wick in the hole in the center of the candle. Trim off the excess.

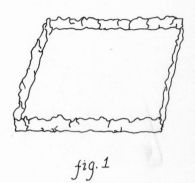

fig. 1

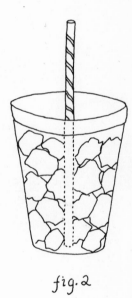

fig. 2

19

Jeweled Candle

Materials:
chopped white wax, 2¼ cups
3⅜ inches of a brightly colored crayon
36-ply cotton twine, 6 inches
sequins
straight pins

Tools:
1-pound can, such as a coffee can,
  bent to form spout
pan of water
9-ounce disposable cup
plastic straw, ⅛ inch in diameter
scissors

Steps:
1. Put the wax pieces and crayon in the can. Set the can in a pan of water, and melt the mixture over very low heat. Be sure an adult is in the room with you when you melt or pour wax.
2. Dip the twine in the wax, and lay it straight on a flat surface to harden. This is the wick.
3. Pour the remaining wax into the disposable cup. Cool until it is thick but still soft.

20

4. Stand the straw in the center of the cup (Figure 1). Be sure it reaches to the bottom.

5. When the candle has cooled enough to be firm but still feels warm, peel off the container. Move the straw gently up and down a few times, and remove it. Turn the candle over.

6. Pin sequins here and there on the candle. Push the pins all the way in. (Figure 2).

7. Insert the wick. Cut off the excess.

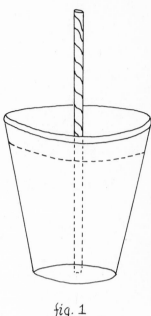

fig. 1

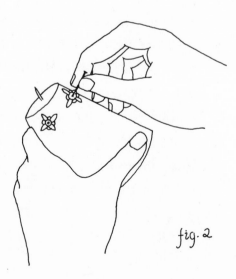

fig. 2

Roll-and-Pinch Candle

Materials:
chopped wax, any color, 1 cup
10-ply cotton twine, 5½ inches

Tools:
1-pound can, such as a coffee can,
    bent to form spout
pan of water
heavy aluminum foil, 6 inches square
table knife

Steps:
1. Put the wax pieces in the can. Set the can in a pan of water, and melt the wax over very low heat. Be sure an adult is in the room with you when you melt or pour wax.

2. Lay the foil on a flat surface, and turn up all edges half an inch (Figure 1). Pour the wax onto the foil. Let the wax thicken and cool until you can work it with your hands.

3. Bend the edges of the foil down. If the edges of the wax are uneven, trim them even with a table knife. Lay the length of twine on the edge of the wax nearest you, with half an inch extend-

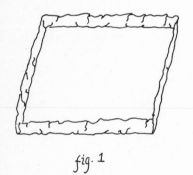

fig. 1

22

ing on one side of the wax. (Figure 2).
4. Roll the edge of the wax over the
twine, pulling the wax loose from the
foil as you roll it (Figure 3). Continue
rolling until all the wax is used. Gently
mold the edges into the cylinder of wax.
Roll it back and forth until the cylinder
is smooth.

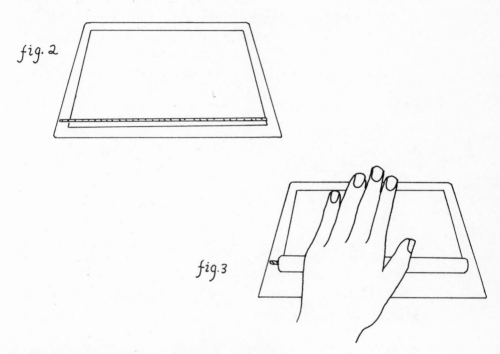

fig. 2

fig. 3

5. Hold the candle so that the wick is
at the top. Gently pinch lowest part of
the candle between your thumb and
forefinger to make an indentation. Now
with your other hand, gently pinch just
above the two indentations on the op-

posite sides. Continue pinching alternate sides all the way up the candle (Figure 4).

6. Repeat, placing thumb and forefinger in the indentations several times, until the candle is almost hard. Put in the refrigerator to finish hardening.

7. To make the candle stand up firmly for burning, drip wax in the center of a saucer and stand the candle in the warm wax.

fig. 4

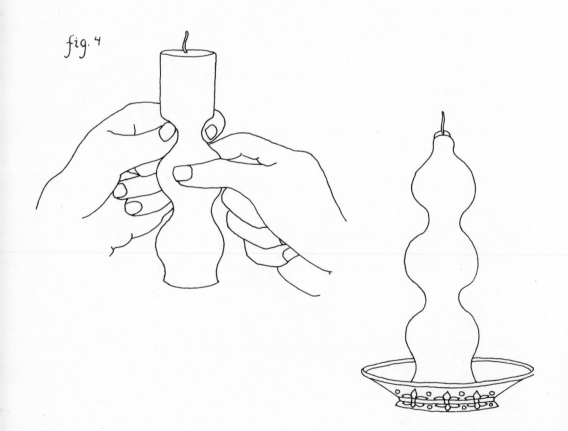

Fourth-of-July Candle

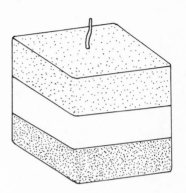

Materials:
chopped white wax, 2⅔ cups
1⅓ inches each of
    red and blue crayon
36-ply cotton twine, 4½ inches

Tools:
3 1-pound cans, such as coffee cans,
    each bent to form spout
pan of water
cream carton, pint size
plastic drinking straw,
    ⅛ inch in diameter
scissors

Steps:
1. Put about one third of the wax in each can. Add red crayon to one and blue crayon to another.
2. Set the can with the blue crayon in a pan of water, and melt the mixture over very low heat. Be sure an adult is in the room with you when you melt or pour wax.
3. Dip the twine in the wax, and lay it straight on a flat surface to harden. This is the wick.

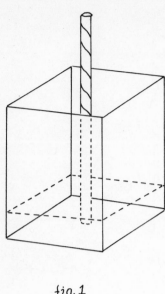

4. Pour the remaining blue wax into the carton. Let it cool until the wax is thick but still soft.

5. Stand the straw in the center of the carton. Be sure it reaches to the bottom (Figure 1).

6. When the blue wax has hardened, repeat the melting, pouring, and hardening with the white wax and then the red wax.

7. Peel off the carton. Move the straw gently up and down a few times. Remove. Insert the wick. Cut off the excess wick.

Dribble Candle

Materials:
chopped wax, any color, $\frac{1}{2}$ cup
10-ply cotton twine, $4\frac{1}{2}$ inches
pop bottle, washed and dried
stub candles, several different colors

Tools:
1-pound can, such as a coffee can,
   bent to form spout
pan of water
heavy aluminum foil, 5 inches square
table knife

Steps:
1. Put the wax pieces in the can. Set the can in a pan of water, and melt the wax over very low heat. Be sure an adult is in the room with you when you melt or pour wax.
2. Lay the foil on a flat surface, and turn up all edges half an inch (Figure 1). Pour the wax on the foil. Let it thicken and cool enough to work with your hands.
3. Bend the edges of the foil down. If the edges of the wax are uneven, trim them even with a table knife. Lay the

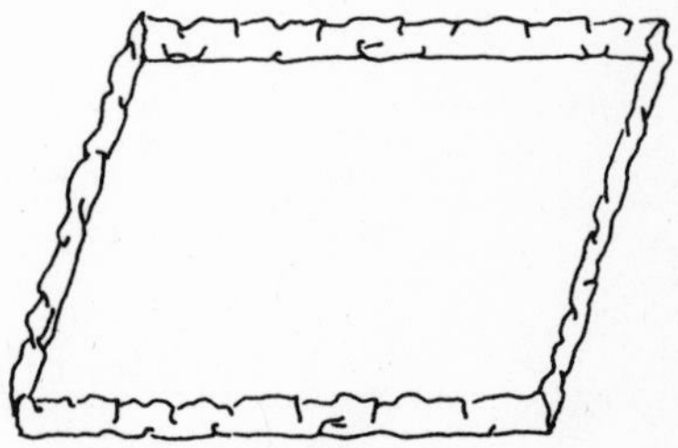

fig. 1

27

length of twine on the edge of the wax nearest you, with a half inch extending out one side of the wax (Figure 2).

4. Roll the edge of the wax over the twine, pulling the wax loose from the foil as you roll it (Figure 3). Continue rolling until all the wax is used. Gently mold the edges into the cylinder of wax. Roll the cylinder back and forth until it is smooth. Lay the candle flat in the refrigerator to harden.

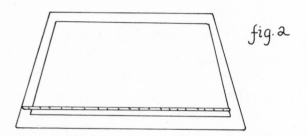

fig. 2

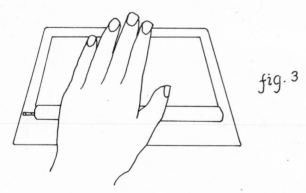

fig. 3

5. Put the bottom half inch of the candle in the top of the bottle. If the candle is too large, trim it to make it fit.

6. Light a stub candle. Hold it horizontally at the top of the candle in the bottle, and let it drip down the sides. Repeat with stub candles of other colors (Figure 4).

7. As your drip candle burns, it will add more drippings to the candle and the bottle.

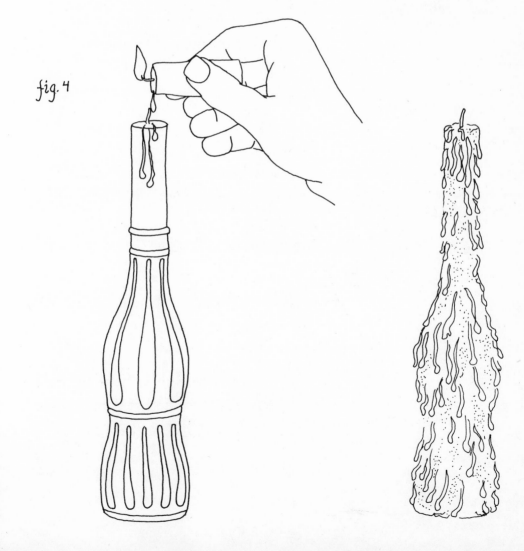

fig. 4

Jack-O'- Lantern

Materials:
white paper
1 tablespoon flour
1½ teaspoons water
6- or 8-ounce clear drinking glass
black enamel paint,
   or one not soluble in water
chopped white wax, 1½ cups
2½ inches of orange crayon
10-ply cotton twine, 6 inches

Tools:
pencil
scissors
paintbrush
1-pound can, such as a coffee can,
   bent to form spout
pan of water
pipe cleaner

Steps:
1. On the paper, draw and cut out several small pumpkins. Draw and cut out eyes, nose, and mouth on each as in the picture (Figure 1). Or draw your own favorite jack-o'-lantern face.
2. Mix the tablespoon of flour and the

fig. 1

teaspoon and a half of water into a
paste. Use it to paste the pumpkins
tightly to various places on the outside
of the drinking glass at least a quarter
of the height from the top (Figure 2).
3. Paint the outside of the glass black,
covering the pumpkins. Let the paint
dry thoroughly.
4. Put the wax pieces and orange
crayon in the can. Set the can in a pan
of water, and melt the mixture over
very low heat. Be sure an adult is in the
room with you when you melt or pour
wax.
5. Dip the twine in the wax, and lay it
straight on a flat surface to harden.
This is the wick.

fig. 2

31

6. Soak the glass in warm water until the paper pumpkins come off (Figure 3). Discard the pumpkins. Pour the water out and dry the glass thoroughly.

7. While the glass is still warm, fill it three-fourths full of wax. Let the wax cool until it is thick but still soft.

8. With a pipe cleaner, make a hole down the center of the glass to the bottom (Figure 4). Insert the wick. Cut off the excess.

fig. 4

Easter Egg

Materials:
chopped white wax, ½ cup
¾ inch of pink crayon
10-ply cotton twine, 3½ inches

Tools:
1 egg
table fork
1-pound can, such as a coffee can,
    bent to form spout
pan of water
egg carton
pipe cleaner
scissors

Steps:
1. Make a hole in the center of the side of the eggshell by tapping with the tip of a fork handle. From around the hole, break off tiny pieces of shell with your fingers or the fork tines until the hole is the size of a penny (Figure 1). Remove the insides of the egg, and save them to use in cooking. Wash the inside of the shell, and let it dry.
2. Put the wax pieces and crayon in the can. Set the can in a pan of water, and

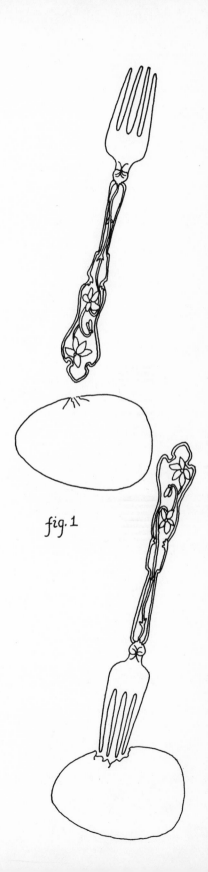

fig. 1

33

melt the wax over very low heat. Be sure an adult is in the room with you when you melt or pour wax.

3. Dip the twine in the wax, and lay it straight on a flat surface to harden. This is the wick.

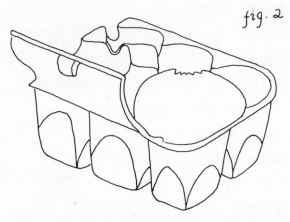

fig. 2

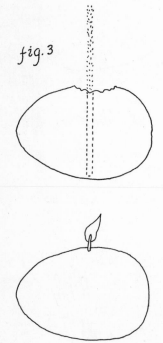

fig. 3

4. Place the eggshell, with the hole on top, in an egg carton so it cannot roll (Figure 2). Pour it full of wax. Let the wax cool until it is thick but still soft.

5. With a pipe cleaner, make a hole through the center of the egg down to the bottom (Figure 3). If wax partially fills the hole, wait a few minutes and remake the hole. Let it harden.

6. Peel off the eggshell. Turn the candle upside down, and insert the wick in the hole. Trim off the excess wick.

34

Topsy-Turvy Candle

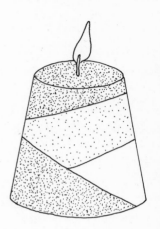

Materials:
chopped white wax, 1¼ cups
1 inch of green crayon
½ inch each of
    orange and yellow crayon
36-ply cotton twine, 5 inches

Tools:
3 1-pound cans, such as coffee cans,
    each bent to form spout
pan of water
5-ounce disposable cup
egg carton
plastic straw, ⅛ inch in diameter
scissors

Steps:
1. Put about half the wax and the green crayon in one can. Divide the remaining wax between the other two cans and add an orange crayon to one and a yellow crayon to the other.
2. Set the can with the green crayon in a pan of water. Melt the mixture over very low heat. Be sure an adult is in the room with you when you melt or pour wax.

3. Dip the twine in the wax, and lay it straight on a flat surface to harden. This is the wick.

4. Pour about half the green wax in the cup. Tip the cup at an angle, and set it in an egg carton (Figure 1). Let the wax cool until it is thick but still soft.

5. Stand the straw in the center of the cup. Be sure the straw stands erect and reaches the bottom of the cup (Figure 2). Leave the cup at an angle until the wax hardens.

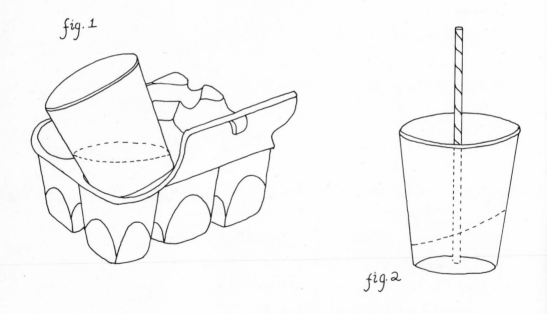

fig. 1

fig. 2

6. Repeat the melting, pouring, and hardening with the orange wax and then the yellow wax, tipping the cup at a different angle for each color but making sure the straw stays erect (Figure 3).

7. Repeat the melting and pouring with the remaining green wax, but let the cup stand straight while the wax hardens (Figure 4).

8. Peel the cup away from the candle. Move the straw gently up and down a few times, and remove it.

9. Turn the candle upside down. Insert the wick in the hole. Trim off the excess wick.

fig. 3

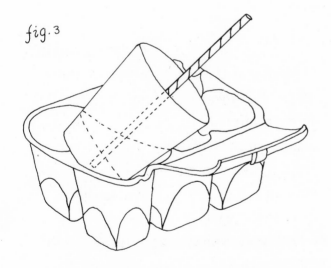

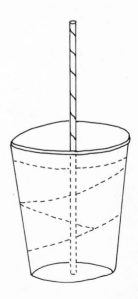

fig. 4

Mushroom Candle

Materials:
chopped white wax, 2 cups
2 inches of pink crayon
36-ply cotton twine, 5 inches

Tools:
1-pound can, such as a coffee can,
   bent to form spout
pan of water
5-ounce disposable cup
plastic straw, ⅛ inch in diameter
teacup with rounded bottom
cooking oil
scissors

Steps:
1. Put the wax pieces and the crayon in the can. Set the can in a pan of water, and melt the wax over very low heat. Be sure an adult is in the room with you when you melt or pour wax.
2. Dip the twine in the wax, and lay it straight on a flat surface to harden. This is the wick.
3. Fill the disposable cup three-fourths full of wax. Let the wax cool until thick but soft.

4. Stand the straw in the center of the disposable cup. Be sure the straw reaches the bottom of the cup (Figure 1). Let the wax harden. Peel off the cup.

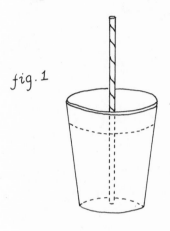

fig. 1

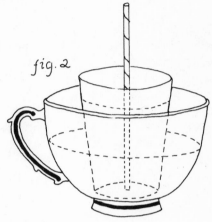

fig. 2

5. Thoroughly oil the inside of the teacup. Place the small end of the candle in the cup (Figure 2).

6. Remelt the remaining wax. Pour it into the teacup. Let the wax harden.

7. Remove the candle gently from the cup. If necessary, set the cup in warm water for a few seconds. Move the straw gently up and down a few times to make a hole in the top of the mushroom. Remove it.

8. Turn the mushroom right side up, and insert the wick in the hole. Cut off the excess.

39

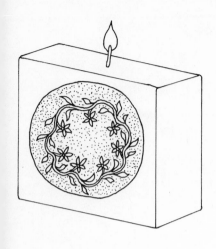

Picture Candle

Materials:
chopped white wax, 3⅓ cups
36-ply cotton twine, 6 inches
⅜ inch of blue crayon
gold paint

Tools:
1-pound can, such as a coffee can,
   bent to form spout
pan of water
cardboard box, such as a small rice box
masking tape
pipe cleaner
cooking oil
heavy aluminum foil, 5 inches square
embossed picture from greeting card
scissors
paintbrush

Steps:
1. Put the wax pieces in the can. Set the can in a pan of water, and melt the wax over very low heat. Be sure an adult is in the room with you when you melt or pour wax.
2. Dip the twine in the wax, and lay it straight on a flat surface to harden. This is the wick.

3. Cut off the box lid. Cover the outside seams of the box with masking tape. Saturate the inside with cooking oil.

4. Pour all but about three tablespoonsful of the wax into the box. Let the wax cool until it is thick but soft.

5. With a pipe cleaner, make a hole through the center to the bottom of the box of wax (Figure 1). Put the wick in the hole.

6. Put the blue crayon in the can with the remaining wax. Set the can in a pan of water, and melt the mixture over very low heat.

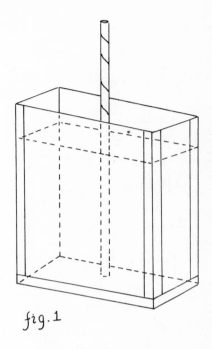

fig. 1

7. Lay the foil on a flat surface, and turn up all edges half an inch. Soak the indented side of the embossed picture with cooking oil, and place it face down on the foil (Figure 2).

8. Pour the blue wax into the indented picture. Be certain the whole picture is covered. Let the wax cool until it is very thick but still soft and pliable.

fig. 2

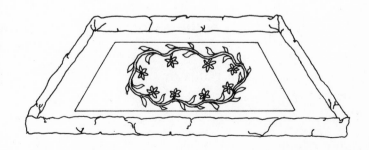

9. Carefully peel the picture away from the wax. Cut around the wax picture in an oval or circle (Figure 3).

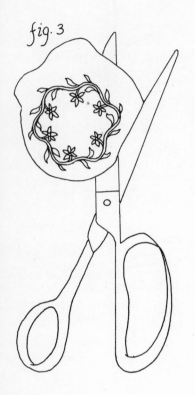

fig. 3

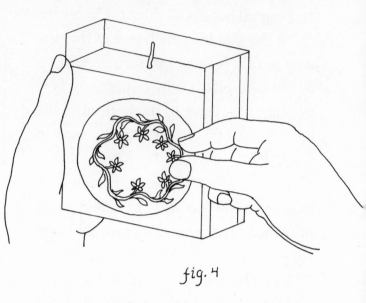

fig. 4

10. While the candle is still slightly warm, peel away one side of the box. With the raised surface outward, place the soft blue wax picture on the center of that side. Press down gently on all edges (Figure 4). Let it harden. Peel away the remainder of the box.

11. Dip the paintbrush in gold paint, wiping it against the inside edge of the bottle several times. Paint the raised part of the wax picture lightly. Let the paint dry.

Ice Candle
with Bell or Ornament

Materials:
small bell or ornament
  (several if you wish)
chopped wax, any color, 2⅔ cups
36-ply cotton twine, 5½ inches

Tools:
5-ounce disposable cup
  (one for each bell or ornament)
1-pound can, such as a coffee can,
  bent to form spout
pan of water
heavy aluminum foil, 6 inches square
table knife
cream carton, pint size
ice chunks

Steps:
1. Put a bell or ornament into a disposable cup. Barely cover it with water (Figure 1). Freeze.
2. Put the wax pieces in the can. Set the can in a pan of water, and melt the wax over very low heat. Be sure an adult is in the room with you when you melt or pour wax.

fig. 1

3. Lay the foil on a flat surface, and turn up all edges half an inch (Figure 2). Pour wax on the foil one eighth of an inch deep. Let the wax thicken and cool enough to work with your hands.
4. Turn the edges of the foil down. If the wax edges are uneven, trim them even with a table knife. Lay the length of twine on the edge of the wax nearest you, with half an inch extending out on one side of the wax (Figure 3).

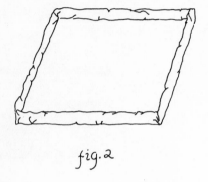

fig. 2

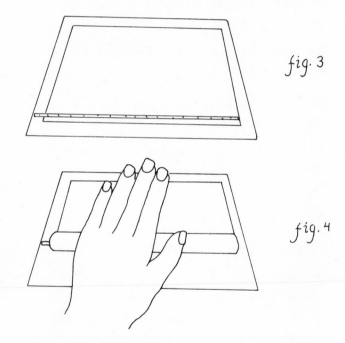

fig. 3

fig. 4

5. Roll the edge of the wax over the twine, pulling the wax loose from the foil as you roll it (Figure 4). Continue rolling until all wax is used. Gently mold the edges into the cylinder of wax. Roll the cylinder back and forth until it is smooth. Lay it flat in the refrigerator to harden.

6. Stand the candle in the center of the pint carton. Drop chunks of ice in the bottom of the carton. Peel the cup from the ice containing the bell or ornament. Put the ice near the outer edge on one side of the carton (Figure 5). Finish filling the carton with ice.

7. Remelt the remaining wax. Pour it into the carton until the carton is almost full. Let the wax harden.

8. Pour out the water left by the melted ice, and peel off the carton.

fig. 5

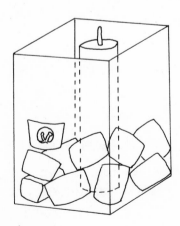 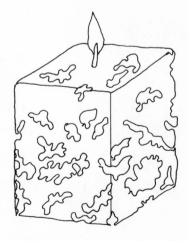

Birthday-Cake Candle

Materials:
chopped white wax, 3 cups
two-inch birthday candles,
   as many as you wish

Tools:
half-gallon plastic bleach bottle
scissors
1-pound can, such as a coffee can,
   bent to form spout
pan of water
cooking oil
table fork
table knife or spatula

Steps:
1. Thoroughly wash the bleach bottle. Cut off the top with scissors, leaving two inches at the bottom (Figure 1). Discard the top. Dry the bottom inside and out.
2. Put the wax pieces in the can. Set the can in a pan of water, and melt the wax over very low heat. Be sure an adult is in the room with you when you melt or pour wax.
3. Thoroughly oil the inside of the

fig. 1

46

bleach bottle. Pour in the wax until it is one inch deep. Let the wax cool until thick but still soft. Insert the birthday candles to the bottom of the bleach bottle (Figure 2). Put the cake in the refrigerator to harden.

4. Bend the edges of the bleach bottle to loosen the candle. If necessary, set it in a pan of warm water for a few seconds. Remove the birthday cake.

5. Remelt the remaining wax. Beat the wax gently with a fork until it is frothy. Spread "frosting" on top and sides of the cake (Figure 3).

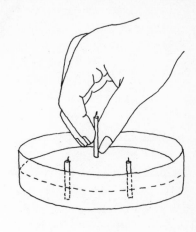

fig. 2

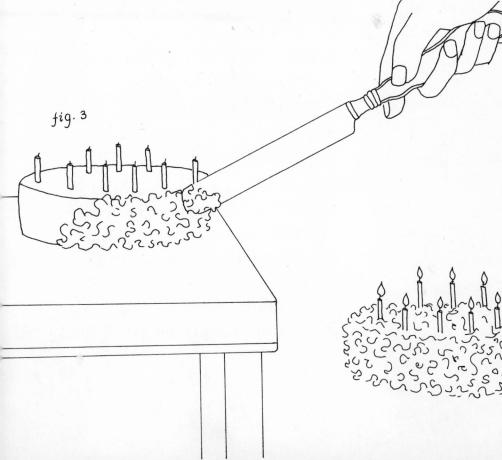

fig. 3

Snowman Candle

Materials:

chopped wax, any dark color,
   3 tablespoons
chopped white wax, 4 cups
36-ply cotton twine, $6\frac{1}{2}$ inches

Tools:

2 1-pound cans, such as coffee cans,
   each bent to form spout
pan of water
1 piece heavy aluminum foil,
   2 inches square
3 pieces heavy aluminum foil,
   each 1 foot square
straight portion cut from coat hanger
   or similar wire, 11 inches
9-ounce disposable cup
scissors

Steps:

1. Put the pieces of dark-colored wax in a can. Set the can in a pan of water, and melt the wax over very low heat. Be sure an adult is in the room with you when you melt or pour wax.

2. Lay the two-inch-square piece of foil on a flat surface, and turn up all edges half an inch (Figure 1). Pour the dark-colored wax into the foil. Let it harden. Break it into tiny pieces.

3. Put the pieces of white wax in a can. Set the can in a pan of water, and melt the wax over very low heat.

4. Dip the twine in the wax, and lay it straight on a flat surface to harden. This is the wick.

5. Lay the three large pieces of foil on a flat surface, and turn up all edges half an inch. Pour about one cup of wax into one piece of foil, about two thirds of a cup in another, and one third in the third (Figure 2). Let the wax thicken and cool enough to work with your hands.

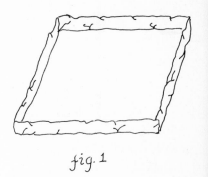

fig. 1

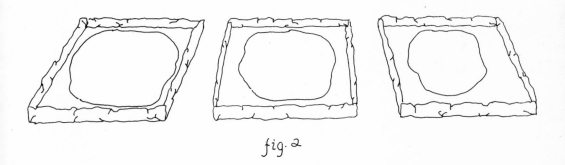

fig. 2

6. Mold the wax into three balls, beginning with the smallest.

49

fig. 3

7. Coat the wire with cooking oil. Turn the disposable cup upside down. Stick the wire into the cup through the center (Figure 3). The cup will hold the wire in place while you make the snowman.
8. Put the center of the largest wax ball on the wire. Slide it down until it rests on the cup (Figure 4). Repeat for the larger of the remaining wax balls and then the smaller. Press the balls gently together so they stick.
9. Stick tiny pieces of dark wax into the top ball for eyes and nose and mouth and into the middle ball for buttons.
10. Rotate the wire a few times, and remove it. Insert the wick. Cut off the excess wick. Put the candle in the refrigerator to finish hardening.

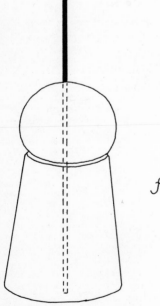

fig. 4

50

Strawberry-Soda Candle

Materials:
white 9-ounce disposable cup
chopped white wax, 2½ cups
3¾ inches of pink crayon
36-ply cotton twine, 7 inches
drinking straw
tiny piece of red crayon

Tools:
1-pound can, such as a coffee can,
    bent to form spout
pan of water
table fork
pipe cleaner
measuring spoon, ¼ or ½ teaspoon size
aluminum foil, 2 inches square
scissors

Steps:
1. Put the wax pieces and the pink crayon in the can. Set the can in a pan of water, and melt the mixture over very low heat. Be sure an adult is in the room with you when you melt or pour wax.
2. Dip the twine in the wax, and lay it straight on a flat surface to harden. This is the wick.

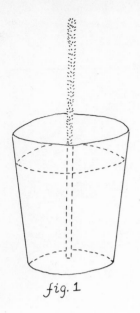

fig. 1

fig. 2

fig. 3

3. Fill the disposable cup three-fourths full of wax. Let the wax cool until it is thick but still soft.

4. With a pipe cleaner, make a hole down the center of the cup to the bottom (Figure 1). Insert the wick in the hole.

5. Set the can with the remaining wax in a pan of water, and melt the wax over very low heat. Turn off the heat, and remove the can to the working area. With a fork, gently beat the wax until it is frothy. Pour it into the disposable cup, heaping it up on top of the cup to look like foam. Leave about one teaspoon of wax in the can.

6. Insert a straw at an angle at the edge of the cup (Figure 2).

7. Set the can with the remaining wax in a pan of water. Add a tiny piece of red crayon. Melt the wax over very low heat.

8. Line the measuring spoon with foil. Pour the red wax into the spoon to make a wax cherry (Figure 3). Let the cherry partially cool. Remove the foil. Put the cherry in the foam, curved side up, near the center. Let it harden.

9. Trim off the excess wick.

Star Candle

Materials:
chopped white wax, ¾ cup
1 inch of blue crayon
10-ply cotton twine, 5 inches

Tools:
2 1-pound cans, such as coffee cans,
    each bent to form spout
pan of water
heavy aluminum foil, 5 inches square
star-shaped cookie cutter
5-ounce disposable cup
scissors

Steps:
1. Put about two thirds of the wax pieces and the blue crayon in one can. Set the can in a pan of water, and melt the mixture over very low heat. Be sure an adult is in the room with you when melt or pour wax.
2. Dip the twine in the wax, and lay it straight on a flat surface to harden. This is the wick.
3. Lay the foil on a flat surface, and set the star cookie cutter on it. Turn up all edges, leaving the foil half an inch

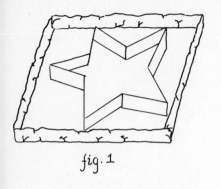

fig. 1

larger in diameter than the cookie cutter (Figure 1). Remove the cookie cutter. Pour wax on the foil about one fourth of an inch deep. Let it cool until it is thick but soft.

4. Lay the wick on the wax, bending the excess up sharply at the edges of the wax (Figure 2). Press the wick down gently with your fingers. Pour on more wax to cover the wick. Let the wax cool until it is thick but soft.

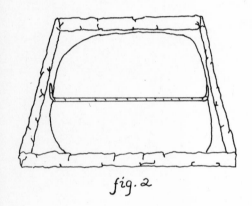

fig. 2

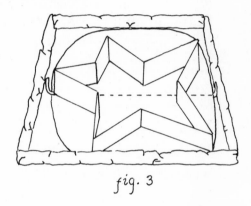

fig. 3

5. Place the star-shaped cutter so that the tip of one star point touches the wick and the other end of the wick extends between two opposite star points (Figure 3). Press down on the cutter. With your fingers, gently remove excess wax, then the cutter. Let the star harden on the foil.

54

6. On two opposite sides of the dispos-able cup, cut ⅜-inch wide slits halfway down (Figure 4).

7. Put the remaining pieces of white wax in the second can. Set the can in a pan of water, and melt the wax over low heat. Pour wax into the cup until it is three eighths of an inch deep. Let it cool until thick but still soft.

fig. 4

8. Cut off the bottom wick at the notch between the star points. Cut off excess wick at the top leaving three eighths of an inch for burning. Put the two bot-tom star points in the cup of white wax. Let the two next higher star points rest in the slits at the sides of the cup to hold the star in place until the wax hardens (Figure 5).

9. Remove the cup.

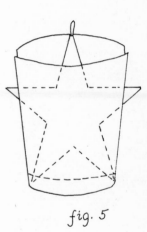

fig. 5

Hamburger Candle

Materials:
chopped white wax, 2 cups
¼ inch of green crayon
2 inches of tan crayon
1 inch of brown crayon
36-ply cotton twine, 4½ inches

Tools:
3 1-pound cans, such as coffee cans,
   each bent to form spout
pan of water
5-ounce disposable cup
2 identical cups with rounded bottoms
cooking oil
pipe cleaner
heavy aluminum foil, 4 inches square
scissors

Steps:
1. Put two tablespoons of wax pieces and the green crayon in one can, one and one third cups of wax pieces and the tan crayon in another, and the remainder of the wax and the brown crayon in the third.
2. Set the can with the green crayon in a pan of water, and melt the mixture

fig. 1

over very low heat. Be sure an adult is in the room with you when you melt or pour wax. Pour the wax into the disposable cup. Let it harden (Figure 1). This is the slice of pickle. Peel away and discard the cup.

3. Set the can with the tan crayon in a pan of water. Melt the mixture over very low heat.

4. Dip the twine in the wax, and lay it straight on a flat surface to harden. This is the wick.

5. Thoroughly oil the insides of the teacups. Pour half the tan wax into each cup. These are the buns. Let them cool until thick but still soft. Make a hole with the pipe cleaner all the way through the center of each bun (Figure 2). If the hole fills with wax, let it cool a little longer and make another hole. Let the wax harden.

fig. 2

6. Set the can with the brown crayon in a pan of water. Melt the mixture over very low heat.

7. Lay the foil on a flat surface, and turn up all edges half an inch (Figure 3). Pour the wax on the foil. Let it thicken and cool enough to work with your hands. Mold it to look like a

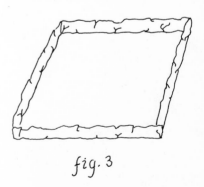

fig. 3

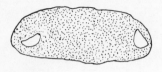

fig. 4

hamburger patty. Break the green wax pickle into two pieces. Push into the hamburger patty near the outer edges (Figure 4).

8. Remove the buns from the teacups. If necessary, set the cups in warm water for a few seconds. If the buns are cold, set them flat side down in a warm pan for a few seconds. Then put the warm hamburger patty inside the buns. Press together gently.

9. Insert a pipe cleaner through the entire hamburger, using the holes already made in the buns and making a hole in the warm hamburger patty. Remove the pipe cleaner and insert the wick. Cut off the excess.

Rocket Candle

Materials:
chopped white wax, 2½ cups
1¼ inches each of
   red and blue crayon
10-ply cotton twine, 10 inches
white candle stub
   or several white birthday candles

Tools:
3 1-pound cans, such as coffee cans,
   each bent to form spout
pan of water
2 pieces heavy aluminum foil,
   each 5½ inches by 9 inches
table knife
cooking oil
cupcake liner
cupcake pan
pipe cleaner
scissors

Steps:
1. Put half the wax pieces into one can, and divide the remaining pieces between the other two cans, adding red crayon to one and blue crayon to the other.

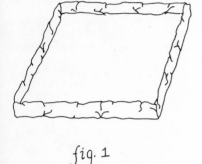

fig. 1

2. Set the can with the white wax in a pan of water, and melt the wax over very low heat. Be sure an adult is in the room with you when you melt or pour wax.

3. Dip the twine in the wax, and lay it straight on a flat surface to harden. Redip, holding the opposite end of the wick. Lay it on a flat surface to harden again.

4. Lay one piece of foil on a flat surface, and turn up all edges half an inch (Figure 1). Pour the wax evenly on the foil. Let the wax thicken and cool enough to work with your hands.

5. Turn the edges of the foil down. If the edges of the wax are uneven, trim them even with a table knife. With the wide edge of the wax facing you, lay the wick on the edge, with half the excess extending over each end (Figure 2).

6. Roll the edge of the wax over the wick, pulling the wax loose from the foil as you roll it (Figure 3). Continue rolling until all the wax is used. Gently mold the edges into the cylinder of wax. Roll the cylinder back and forth until it is smooth. Lay it flat in the refrigerator to harden.

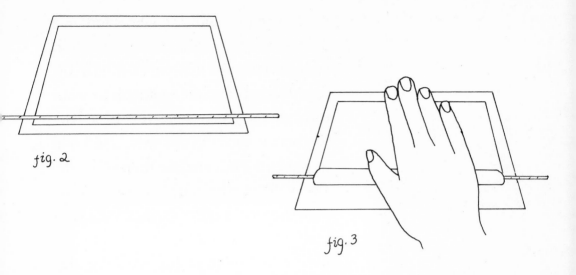

fig. 2

fig. 3

7. Set the can of wax with the red crayon in a pan of water, and melt the mixture over very low heat. Oil the cupcake liner, and put it in the cupcake tin. Pour in the wax. Let it cool until thick but still soft.

8. With a pipe cleaner, make a hole through the center of the cake to the bottom (Figure 4). If the hole fills with wax, let it cool some more and make another hole. Let it harden. Remove the cupcake liner.

9. Set the can with the blue crayon in a pan of water, and melt the mixture over very low heat.

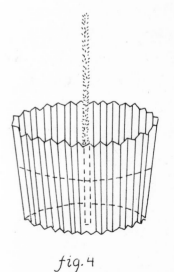

fig. 4

10. Put the remaining piece of foil on a flat surface, and turn up all edges half an inch. Pour the wax onto the foil, and let it thicken and cool enough to work with your hands. Mold it into a ball. Flatten the ball on one side, and mold it into a point on the opposite side. This will be the rocket head.

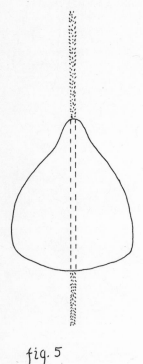

fig. 5

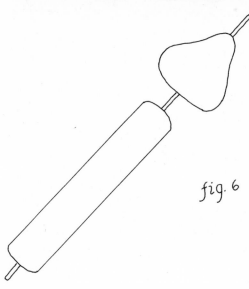

fig. 6

11. When the head is firm enough to hold its shape, make a hole with a pipe cleaner through the center of the tip and out the center of the flat part (Figure 5). Insert one end of the wick from the white cylinder up through the hole (Figure 6). Mold the blue wax firmly against the white cylinder.

12. Turn the red wax cupcake upside down. Thread the remaining end of the wick from the white cylinder through the hole. Hold the wick loosely at the bottom of the candle while someone drips wax from the stub candle onto the center of the red wax (Figure 7).

13. Join the red and white sections. Hold them firmly together while someone drips white wax all around the place where the parts join. Let the joint harden. Trim the excess wick.

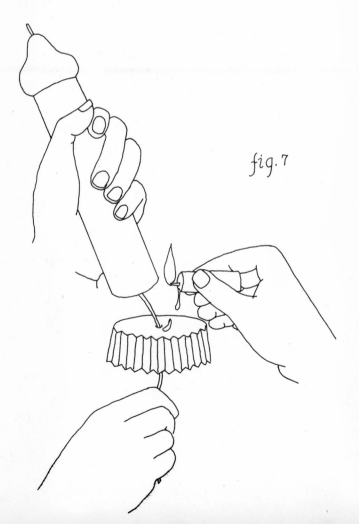

fig. 7

Conclusion

After you have made these candles, try other color combinations and other molds. Try shaping warm wax with your fingers much the same way as you would shape clay. When you form a shape that pleases you, use a pipe cleaner to make a hole in the warm wax. Then insert a wick, and you have a special candle creation. After making candles, there still remains the fun and satisfaction of watching the soft glow as they burn, or of giving them as special one-of-a-kind gifts.